TAYLOR SWIFT

UNOFFICIAL

Publisher and Creative Director: Nick Wells
Project Editor: Polly Prior
Art Director: Mike Spender
Layout Design: Jane Ashley
Digital Design and Production: Chris Herbert

Special thanks to: Laura Bulbeck, Emma Chafer, Esme Chapman,
Karen Fitzpatrick, Dawn Laker, Daniela Nava

FLAME TREE PUBLISHING
Crabtree Hall, Crabtree Lane
Fulham, London SW6 6TY
United Kingdom
www.flametreepublishing.com

Website for this book: www.flametreepop.com

First published 2013

13 15 17 16 14
1 3 5 7 9 10 8 6 4 2

A CIP record for this book is available from the British Library upon request.

ISBN 978-0-85775-865-1

Printed in China

TAYLOR SWIFT

UNOFFICIAL

Alice Hudson
Foreword by Kate Lucey

**FLAME TREE
PUBLISHING**

Contents

Foreword

5

Country Sweetheart

6

All American Girl

25

Living The Dream

39

Further Information

48

Biographies & Picture Credits

48

Foreword

Taylor Swift makes me feel a little bit sick. At the ripe age of 23 she's achieved more than most musicians hope for in their entire career; she's had a string of gorgeous boyfriends; is always charming and polite, and she's got really lovely hair.

Her anecdotal tales of sleuthing ex-lovers sung to incessantly catchy melodies have made her a global superstar, and you'll never see her falling out of a club or a cab with her 'Swift' on display, or on the front of a magazine with her 'Taylors' out. We write about Taylor a lot at Sugarscape.com, and the most shocking thing in her career history (aside from some of her boyfriend choices) was when she started to wear her hair straight instead of curly. HUGE. DEAL.

In person, Taylor is composed, collected and in control of everything – unlike some other celebrities who seem to be schlepped about from place to place without much of a say or clue. Though – as you might expect from someone who had as tough a time in school as Taylor did – she seems very self aware.

Swifty is the ultimate girls' girl – we love her fashion sense, her music and her attitude. With such glittering reviews across the world, it's hard to believe some of the struggles she's been through that we come across in this book: Tay-Swizzle wasn't always loved and adored by everyone. Staying strong and learning how to stand up in the face of negativity doubtlessly helped her take over the world with her guitar, and turn it into something positive – like a fat bank balance. There comes that sick feeling again.

Kate Lucey

Editor, Sugarscape.com

5

Country Sweetheart

Ever-polite and charming to journalists and the public alike, Taylor is intelligent and sweet natured. That's unless, of course, you are an ex-boyfriend who has wronged her, in which case you can expect to feature in a song – and it probably won't be complimentary. Although she may be a nice person and a good role model to hordes of young, adoring fans, Taylor is a smart, savvy businesswoman. Her romantic ideals may reside somewhere up in the clouds, yet her feet are firmly planted on the ground.

Is it her childlike excitement that makes her endearing? Perhaps it's her wit and sense of humour – she always has a smile on her face and isn't afraid to laugh at herself. What's certain is that Taylor Swift has the rare ability to connect immediately with almost everyone she meets – including, most importantly, her fans.

'I've loved my fans from the very first day … [they] make me feel like they're my friends – more now than ever before. I'll never go a day without thinking about our memories together.'

Taylor Swift

Solid Platinum

Taylor Swift fills venues, sells records and sings about break-ups like no other. Undoubtedly, she's one of the hottest acts on the planet. At just 23, the sweet-natured yet savvy American singer-songwriter has released four multiplatinum-selling studio albums, undertaken three sell-out world tours and amassed a gigantic fortune.

The country crooner turned-mainstream-megastar is one of only a handful of music acts able to sell out the biggest stadiums – in, usually, between one and three minutes. Decibel levels reached by the hordes of screaming fans have been compared to the hysteria of 'Beatlemania'. Incredibly, each night on tour is worth over US$1 million.

'My favorite thing in life is writing about life, specifically the parts of life concerning love. Because, as far as I'm concerned, love is absolutely everything.'

Taylor Swift

'It's like a message in a bottle. You can put this message in a bottle, throw it out into the ocean, and maybe someday, the person that you wrote that song about is going to hear it and understand exactly how you felt.'

Taylor Swift

Sing Out, Sister

A big part of Taylor's appeal is down to her seemingly natural songwriting capabilities. She is a quick-witted lyricist, willing to share personal details – primarily relating to love, longing and failed romances – via her words. Her detail-laden, narrative songs resonate with a wide range of people, although her most die-hard fans are generally tweens and teens, particularly girls.

Hard Graft

Taylor Swift is highly regarded by fans and critics alike for her all-round musicianship. With an innate ability to come up consistently with classy lyrics, killer hooks and catchy melodies, Swift can play the ukelele, banjo and piano, although the instrument she cherishes the most, aside from her voice, is the guitar.

Taylor's success wouldn't have come without dogged determination and a burning ambition to make it. For as long as she can remember, she has wanted to be on stage. She worked hard towards what she wanted with a focus rarely seen in one so young. In a clip recorded before the release of her first album, country's most successful crossover star spoke of her long-held dream: to get up on a stage and look out to a crowd of thousands, who already know the words to her songs.

Coming Of Age

'I was never convinced I was going to make it,' Swift admitted to National Public Radio in 2012. For a girl so eager and productive, it felt as though time was somehow running out. So it was a relief for Taylor to get debut single 'Tim McGraw' out to the public's ears in 2006, as well as the rest of *Taylor Swift*, her first album, described by the singer as 'the diary of when I was 14, 15, 16'.

Liz Rose is named as co-writer on seven tracks; Taylor, naturally, is listed on them all. Initially, she had worked with several producers on the album, but ultimately she felt she 'gelled' best with Nathan Chapman, who produced her demo. The tenacious teen managed to convince the label to hire Chapman, even though he'd never produced a studio album before.

'Be that strong girl that everyone knew would make it through the worst, be that fearless girl ... be that independent girl who didn't need a man ... who never backed down.'

Taylor Swift

15

'When someone apologizes to you enough times for things they'll never stop doing, I think it's Fearless to stop believing them. It's Fearless to say "you're not sorry" and walk away.'

Taylor Swift

'Tim McGraw'

'Tim McGraw' was Taylor's first single, released on 19 June 2006. Taylor wrote this song during her freshman year of high school, knowing that she and her then-boyfriend – a senior – would break up when he left for college. The singer said she wanted her ex 'to be reminded of me'. Lyrically, the song evokes those moments which Taylor thinks should remind him of her – one being the Tim McGraw song, 'Can't Tell Me Nothing' from the country star's *Live Like You Were Dying* album.

The track performed well, reaching No. 40 on the Billboard Hot 100 and being certified platinum, although it was the country charts, naturally, that registered the most success, with the track peaking at No. 6 on the Hot Country Songs chart. The album's four other singles, 'Teardrops On My Guitar', 'Our Song', 'Picture to Burn' and 'Should've Said No' went platinum too. 'Our Song' became Swift's first No. 1 on Hot Country Songs.

From The Heart

Taylor's second studio album was confirmation that the singer had successfully genre-hopped her way into the mainstream – in a big way. By 2013, *Fearless*, featuring 13 love and heartbreak-inspired tracks penned by Swift, had sold over 10 million copies worldwide. It's also the only album to spend a full year in the Billboard 200. *Fearless* saw the young singer hold on to her country audience whilst adding multitudes of new 'pop' and 'pop/rock' listeners to an ever-expanding fanbase. The album also marked her record producing debut.

'And you'll add my name to your long list of traitors who don't understand/And I'll look back and regret how I ignored when they said/'Run as fast as you can.'

Taylor Swift singing about John Mayer

('Dear John' lyrics)

Awarded To You

With her string of hits, Taylor saw the plaudits and nominations begin to roll in. 'Tim McGraw' won her a BMI Award for songwriting and Breakthrough Video of the Year at the fan-voted CMT Music Awards, whilst she scooped the Horizon Award for Best New Artist at the Country Music Association Awards (CMAs). She was also nominated for an American Country Music Award (ACM) and an American Music Award (AMA) and was honoured by the Nashville Songwriter's Association International as Songwriter/Artist of the Year 2007. *Taylor Swift* ended 2007 as the top-selling country album of that year.

Rolling Stone observed that one of the keys to her success was her ability to expand the demographic of country to include suburban adolescent girls. Taylor achieved this by way of her confessional-style teen diary lyrics, combined with a skilful use of social media, which the magazine noted was 'unprecedented' within the genre.

'Swift might be a clever Nashville pro who knows all the hitmaking tricks, but she's also a high-strung, hyper-romantic gal with a melodramatic streak the size of the Atchafalaya Swamp.'

Rolling Stone

Grammy Girl

You couldn't blame Taylor for losing track of how many industry accolades she has won or the number of times she has entered the record books. Of 190 nominations, Taylor has come away the winner more than two thirds of the time, collecting 119 gongs. In 2009, aged just 20, she became the youngest person in history to take the gong for Album of the Year at the Grammy Awards. She has since collected five more of the trophies, together with a string of other awards for her performances, videos, singles, albums and sales. Swift's two latest records, *Speak Now* (2010) and *Red* (2012), both sold over a million copies within their first seven days of release, smashing records. By its third week, *Red* had topped the charts in 42 countries, with sales headed towards two million. Taylor now holds the worldwide record for 'career sales', currently sitting at more than 26 million albums and 75 million song downloads.

'The blue-eyed teenage bombshell writes
her own songs, plays guitar, and drops
boy-crazed salvos while working a brutally
honest, vulnerable side that gives her hyper-
professional craft an autobiographical edge.'
Rolling Stone bio

All American Girl

Taylor Alison Swift was born in Reading, Pennsylvania, on 13 December 1989. Her father Scott is a stockbroker, whereas her mother quit her job as a mutual fund marketing executive to be a housewife. Taylor was named after the singer, James Taylor, a favourite of her mother's, although Andrea Swift also wanted Taylor to have a name that was gender neutral, as she thought it would help her get ahead, particularly career-wise.

Taylor credits her mother with giving her the confidence to succeed in life: 'Mom is calculated, logical, business-minded; kind but very, very direct.' She remembers Andrea's diligence in helping her prepare for class presentations, the pair staying up all night to run through different ideas. Taylor shares an equally close relationship with her father. 'My dad is … the social butterfly; friendly … tells me that every performance is the greatest he's ever seen, every new outfit is the coolest. Constant cheerleader,' she enthuses. Taylor also has a good relationship with brother Austin, whom she has often turned to for advice on her latest crush.

'I look at this young woman and everything

she's accomplished and where she is and yet

I still see that little girl in the car seat with

those big blue eyes in my rear view mirror.

I say, "That's my baby and I'm real proud."'

Andrea Swift

Schooldays

Taylor attended the private Wyndcroft School until the age of nine, when the family moved to Wyomissing, Pennsylvania. There, Taylor attended West Reading Elementary Center and Wyomissing Area Junior/Senior High School. It was during middle school that Taylor became targeted by the school bullies. It was her country music hobby which made her stand out and initially attracted negative attention.

'So … middle school? Awkward … Singing the national anthem on weekends instead of going to sleepovers? More awkward. Braces? Awkward. Gain a lot of weight before you hit the growth spurt? Awkward. Frizzy hair, don't embrace the curls yet? Awkward. Try to straighten it? Awkward!' she recounted, laughing, to *Vogue*.

In typical Taylor fashion, she wrote songs about her feelings – and wow, how that paid off.

Once Taylor had decided to pursue music seriously, she was home-schooled for her high-school junior and senior years.

Along The Country Road

Evidence of Taylor's love of romantic songs can be found in the Swift family home movie collection. One clip features Taylor singing her version of 'Unchained Melody', by The Righteous Brothers – aged just two. 'My whole life I've loved music,' she told Oprah Winfrey. 'I would see all these people on big stages and I didn't think I could do that … I just loved music.' A bright kid, Taylor's talent for putting words together revealed itself initially through poetry.

'I noticed early on that poetry was something that just stuck in my head,' she recalls. In fourth grade, Swift wrote a three-page poem, called 'Monster in My Closet', winning a national poetry contest.

She was always singing and writing; family friend Angel Helm recalled a young Taylor singing on the beach during summer, penning lyrics too. One year, aged about 12, she devoted the whole summer to writing a 350-page novel.

'I haven't had that one great love, which is good. I don't want that to be in the past; I want it to be in the future.'

Taylor Swift

The Magical Land of Nashville

Taylor's parents began ferrying their determined daughter to and from Nashville; initially, they approached label reps themselves but were then advised that a respected manager was required. This is how the Swifts ended up securing a meeting with one of Britney Spears' representatives: New York-based agent Dan Dymtrow. Recognizing Taylor's potential, he used his contacts to get her in front of key record executives. The eighth grader was offered an RCA artist development deal; in typical Taylor-speak, the singer later described this contract as an 'in-between record deal, like a guy who says he wants to date you, but not be your boyfriend'.

Big Machine Gets Taylor

In 2005 Swift performed during an industry showcase at Nashville's Bluebird Café. DreamWorks executive Scott Borchetta was there and he later claimed that her music just 'hit' him. He sought Swift and her parents out after the show and they all warmed to him straight away. Taylor later recalled Scott as saying, 'The good news is I want you on my record label; the bad news is I don't actually have a record label yet. But please wait for me.' Even though – as Taylor puts it in the 'Journey to Fearless' documentary – 'he only had the dream, no name, no building, no staff,' she liked and trusted Borchetta and decided to go with her gut. Months later she became one of the first artists to sign to Big Machine Records.

'I genuinely felt that I was running out of time. I wanted to capture these years of my life on an album while they still represented what I was going through.'

Taylor on walking out on RCA

Who Do You Love?

Taylor's sound is a fusion of country-pop-rock, resulting from a wide range of musical influences throughout her life. As a young girl, Taylor's first ever music idol was her grandmother, Marjorie Finlay: a former opera singer. Taylor told Country Music Television (CMT), 'She was always singing, either around the house, or every single Sunday she'd get up and sing in front of the entire congregation at church' – something the youngster found 'thrilling'. As a toddler, 'Tay Tay' also adored Disney movie soundtracks. 'I would come out of Disney movies singing the entire songs, and my parents were like, "Didn't you just hear that once?"' Her parents also noticed it didn't matter if tiny Taylor forgot the words to a song – she'd simply make up her own.

Somewhat surprisingly, Swift is also a hip-hop fan – she loves the rhyming patterns, particularly those of artists such as Eminem. She told *Rolling Stone*, 'Country and hip-hop are two of the most honest genres because we just like to sing about our lifestyle ... Pride is something that both country and hip-hop share.'

'There is really no feeling like the feeling you get after you finish a song and you sit there and you just think: that is exactly how I felt.'

Taylor Swift

From Girl to Goddess

Taylor first burst on to the scene as a fresh-faced teen with unruly blonde waves. Back then, she wore a near-uniform of sundress and cowboy boots - even to awards shows. Red-lipped retro was her next look. Taylor can be held singularly responsible for bringing high-waisted, full skirts back into fashion. Of late, she appears to have morphed into a sleek, designer-clad, Amazonian goddess with more than a tad of Jackie O chic thrown into the fashion mix. Swift can regularly be seen on best-dressed lists the world over, and has appeared on the covers of dozens of fashion magazines.

By her own admission, Taylor is 'like, totally a dress girl' who has always favoured an ultra-feminine look. She is able to pull off red-carpet glamour with ease. Taylor also adores fancy dress, as well as dressing up, and she is unapologetically in love with glitter and sequins – particularly favouring them whilst performing those hair-tossing routines during her live shows.

'It never mattered to me that people in school didn't think that country music was cool … it did matter to me that I was not wearing the clothes that everybody was wearing at that moment.

Swift talks to Vogue

Like Her? Love Her!

The love Taylor's fans have for the star is matched by what she feels for them – in fact, she may love them even more. Extremely business-savvy, the 23-year-old, who is CEO of her own management company, knows the power that her fanbase holds in terms of selling records. Her fans enjoy top treatment and treats from the star – not because she is trying to buy their loyalty but because that's the sort of person she is: giving, loving and grateful. She has said that ensuring her fans' happiness is top of her priority list.

Taylor greets fans before and after every single show, and her concerts are designed so that she can get amongst the audience as much as possible. During the Fearless tour, she performed part of the concert at the back of the venue, delighted those in the 'cheap seats' and did a lengthy walk through the crowd, hugging and touching dozens of lucky fans every night.

'I've wanted one thing for my whole life and I'm not going to be that girl who wants one thing her whole life then gets it and complains.'

Taylor Swift, talking about fame

Living The Dream

Following the international success of her third album *Speak Now* in 2010, Taylor released the sensational No. 1 hit 'We Are Never Ever Getting Back Together' from the album *Red* (2012). As well as showing a different style – of dress and image in the popular video – the song and the album show that Swift is developing as a songwriter and is, of course, beginning to grow up. She's still singing about boys, but her outlook on love is getting, well, more realistic. Other hits from the album are 'Begin Again' (for country radio), 'I Knew You Were Trouble' and '22'.

'She has rocketed to the top of the music industry but still keeps her feet on the ground, [she's] shattered every expectation of what a 22-year-old can accomplish.'
Michelle Obama, First Lady

Taylor Made For Success

Taylor's momentum never seems to slow: in December 2011 she unveiled 'Safe & Sound', a collaboration with The Civil Wars for *The Hunger Games* film soundtrack; the latter also features Swift's recording of 'Eyes Open'.

In October 2012, the release of her fourth album *Red* made headlines the world over and again saw Taylor break multiple records for its incredible sales (1.2 million in the first week and nearly 2 million three weeks in). The first week sales were the biggest seen in a decade since Eminem's *The Eminem Show* (2002). Taylor, of course, was over the moon and disbelieving: 'They just told me Red sold 1.2 million albums first week. How is this real life?! You are UNREAL. I love you so much. Thanks a million ;),' she tweeted on hearing the news.

And Still Time For All This?

From country music wannabe, to pop music superstar, there's no doubt the determined and talented Miss Taylor Swift was born to perform – and to write chart-storming songs! Yet there's much more to this self-described 'girls' girl' than meets the eye. A smart businesswoman, Taylor's more than comfortable sitting at the boardroom table as CEO of her own management company. The singer has entered into several lucrative contracts with major brands, including an endorsement deal with CoverGirl makeup, Sony, American Greetings, a clothing line called l.e.i sold in Walmart and a series of deals with mega chain store Target, giving it rights to sell special editions of her records. 'One of the toughest things about putting together an album is having to make the final song choices,' Swift says in a PR statement. 'I love that putting out a Deluxe Edition at Target lets me give the fans even more music.'

'Being 22, you're kind of in a crash course with love and life and lessons and learning the hard way, and thankfully, I've been able to write about those emotions as they've affected me.'

Taylor Swift

On The Road

Taylor Swift is not the sort of girl who does things by halves. That applies, in particular, to her live concerts, which feature a strong theatrical element. The Fearless tour was a cultural phenomenon in terms of its popularity and scale. Taylor sold out all her venues in minutes, including the massive stadiums: LA's Staples Center tickets went in two minutes, whilst Madison Square Garden sold out in under 60 seconds. Her Speak Now tour was another giant and successful spectacle, with 111 dates, in Asia, Europe, North America and Australasia, running between February 2011 and March 2012.

The Red tour has also been a sell out in 2013 – 64 North American dates span from March to September 2013, which include 13 stadium performances. Big names (Nelly, B.o.B Train and Neon Trees) take to the stage with Taylor for duets at various dates, while Ed Sheeran appears as a support act – apparently the two are in cahoots to write material together in the future.

And it seems that she's also in demand from fellow musicians, too: in June 2013, she joined legendary rockers The Rolling Stones on stage in Chicago, where she sang a version of the band's 1964 hit 'As Tears Go By' with Mick Jagger, to the great delight of the Stones' fans. The second leg of her Red tour takes place in Australia and New Zealand from November to December 2013.

Hollywood Beckons

She's got enough Grammys; has Taylor now got her eye on an Oscar? The singer is no stranger to acting, having appeared in an episode of CSI and in friend Miley Cyrus's film *Hannah Montana: The Movie* (2009). She also played the high school sweetheart of former real-life flame, Taylor Lautner in *Valentine's Day* (2010) and voiced the character Audrey in the Dr Seuss adaptation, *The Lorax* (2012). It's been reported that Taylor has signed on to play singer Joni Mitchell in the upcoming movie, *Girls Like Us*, based on the book of the same name by Sheila Weller. She's already got the house in LA, having purchased a US$3.5 million home in Beverley Hills in 2011; in the same year, she also splashed out on a US$2.5 million historic estate for her parents in Nashville, and in 2013 paid US$17 million in cash for her latest pad, a beachfront mansion in Rhode Island.

'Getting your heart broken is worth 4–5 albums! So I try to look on the bright side … you've had your heart broken: it's sad but it's very productive!'
Taylor jokes with Paul O'Grady

A Good Girl

Her intelligence, maturity and strong sense of responsibility make it no surprise to find Taylor an influential philanthropist who has given millions to numerous charities with a focus on those for sick children, children's literacy, LGBT rights and natural disaster relief. She has also been actively involved in Global Youth Service Day and has headed a campaign to protect children from online predators.

Who knows what Taylor will do next? Her dreams have come true, yet there's plenty of time to make new ones. The girl loves her life, yet still has worries like anyone else, and it's refreshing to hear a star talk about both sides of the coin. When Oprah asked her whether fame was what she had expected it to be like, she laughed and blurted out, 'It's better!'

Taylor Swift Vital Info

Birth Name	Taylor Alison Swift
Date of birth	13 December 1989
Birthplace	Reading, Pennsylvania, US
Nationality	American
Height	1.80 m (5 ft 11 in)
Hair Colour	Blonde
Eye Colour	Blue

Online

taylorswift.com:	Official website packed with information including tour dates, Taylor's blog, fan forums and an online store
taylorswiftweb.net:	One of the first and most updated unofficial fan sites; with plenty of news, forums and extensive photo galleries
@taylorswift13:	Join millions of others and follow Taylor's very own Twitter updates
facebook.com/TaylorSwift:	Head to Taylor's Facebook page to meet other fans and access exclusive up-to-date postings
myspace.com/taylorswift:	Listen to Taylor's songs, albums and playlists – for free!
youtube.com/artist/taylor-swift:	Head to Taylor's official YouTube channel to watch her music videos and interviews
flametreepop.com:	Celebrity, fashion and pop news, with loads of links, downloads and free stuff!

Acknowledgements

Alice Hudson (Author)

From New Zealand, Alice fused twin passions for writing and music while a student, reviewing and interviewing international bands and DJs. She is currently based in London, writing and researching for corporate clients across a wide range of sectors, from health and fitness and financial services, to social media and entertainment.

Kate Lucey (Foreword)

Kate Lucey is a celebrity and entertainment journalist, working heavily across pop music as editor of Sugarscape.com. From measuring the hair of One Direction and touring the world with Rihanna, to trying to convince A-Listers to let her sniff them, she's pretty much seen it all. Kate's steered Sugarscape through some phenomenal growth (over 10 million monthly page impressions) and was shortlisted for PPA's New Editor of the Year 2013.

Picture Credits

All images © **Getty Images**: FilmMagic: 18, front cover & 23, 30, 45; Getty Images Entertainment: 1, 3, 21, 26, 29, 38, 42; Getty Images for Clear Channel: 7, 8, 37, 47; Getty Images for MTV: 15; WireImage: 11, 12 & back cover, 16, 24, 33, 41.